CAROLINE Fibæk

*Raw*Cakes

Magic Healthy Cakes

Grub Street ★ London

Published in 2014 by
Grub Street
4 Rainham Close
London SW11 6SS

Email:food@grubstreet.co.uk
Web: www.grubstreet.co.uk
Twitter: @grub_street

A CIP catalogue entry for this book is available from the British Library.

ISBN 978-1-909808-16-4

Printed in Slovenia

CONTENTS

For all the cool women (and their men) who deserve life's sweetness, filled with nutrition, vitamins and energy. And most important of all WITHOUT FEELING GUILTY!

Welcome to the sweet life

Most people believe that living healthily means a life of self-denial. But a life without sugar, cakes, sweets and everything that your taste buds normally crave will make even the most fanatical health enthusiast give in to chocolate, cakes and similar decadence.

That is why I have written this book. The book is for you who hate diets, but love good food and want a healthy life with lots of indulgences. Healthy living is not only about diets and finger wagging. Healthy living is also about playing and loving life and your body.

The recipes in this book contain no sugar, gluten, dairy products, additives or animal fats. They are 100 % vegan, not heat treated, and they are all natural and full of flavour and nourishment. These cakes and desserts prove that you do not need to sacrifice flavour or style in order to be healthy.

And of course you do not need to be a raw foodie. The cakes in this book are perfect for children's birthday parties, for nurseries that have banned sugar, for people with allergies or diabetes and of course for all of us who simply like cakes but don't want to slacken our demands for quality and health.

Most of the cakes in this book can be made with ordinary kitchen equipment, but you will probably come across a number of ingredients that perhaps you would not normally stock in your kitchen. In the next pages I will therefore explain a little bit more about the special ingredients I use for adding flavour, colour and texture to the cakes. At the back of the book you will also find a list of stockists in order that you may easily and quickly find your new ingredients.

Most people will be able to learn to live healthily, since we all know perfectly well that a carrot is healthier than an ice-cream cone with topping. The problem is to stay focused on your health goal – also when life is against you and you just want to throw yourself on the sofa with the TV and a plate of cakes. That is what I call comfort cakes.

'What you resist persists' is my motto. Since the forbidden will somehow one way or another always be more alluring. Instead of banning temptations in your life, you should try to upgrade your (bad) habits. Find a healthier alternative and be prepared. Life is too short to feel guilty!

What is raw food?

Raw food is about eating as naturally as possible. The theory is that in order to get a live body you have to fill it with live food.

Raw food is unprocessed food which is eaten raw or heated to a maximum of 42°C and therefore maintains its optimum nutritional value. Raw food is fresh fruit and vegetables, seeds, nuts, sprouts, kernels, beans, algae, seaweed, vegetable oils, honey and super foods, and raw food is a fabulous way of adding to the body not only vitamins and minerals, but also enzymes, antioxidants and essential fats.

If you convert your diet to raw food you will quickly experience a sense of well being. Your skin will be more beautiful, you will have stronger nails and hair and your eyes will be clearer. You will lose excess kilos and you will get a better muscle tone while at the same time bad breath and body odour will disappear.

But you will also experience a psychological gain in the form of having more energy, more focus and better overview. You will experience that you are better able to concentrate, you will sleep better and your memory will improve. In other words you will have more joy, surplus and balance in your daily life.

No dietary supplement or ready made dishes can compare with the life force of fresh, raw fruit and vegetables; raw food is used in the treatment of a number of ailments, amongst others, allergy, eczema, skin problems, being overweight, diabetes, asthma, arthritis, hormonal imbalances, a weakened immune system and in some cases even cancer.

And then raw food is good for the environment. Growing vegetables and fruit trees is far more sustainable and much better for our planet's eco systems than animal production, which has proven to be the bigger sinner, both when it comes to CO_2 emission, use of water and energy, cutting down vital forests and de-mineralizing and destruction of the soil.

The cakes in this book are all prepared on the raw food principles, which for me is the supreme form of health. I hope you will enjoy the cakes as much as I have enjoyed creating them!

Caroline Fibæk

Eat like you give a damn!

Gear and gadgets

Most of the cakes can be made with ordinary kitchen equipment but some of them require a little extra equipment. Therefore you will find in front of every recipe a symbol for the equipment you will need – in order that you may easily and quickly make a start.

List of symbols

 Blender

 Food processor

 Coffee grinder

 Dehydrator

 Grater

 Ice maker

 Spring forms, cake tins and cutters

BLENDER
It is important to have a good blender. I use a VitaMix – the king of blenders. But cheaper ones will also do. The most important feature to look for in a blender is power (a VitaMixer has 2 hp) so it will be able to blend nuts and make them creamy. I use my VitaMixer for almost everything, both for chopping nuts really finely, blending dates for mash and to make nut cream.

FOOD PROCESSOR
Magimix is without a doubt the Rolls-Royce of food processors. It can grate, slice, chop, blend, pulse and purée. And unlike blenders a food processor does not need water to be able to operate. A food processor is particularly good for making cake bases. But it is not so well suited for making nut cream.

COFFEE GRINDER
A coffee grinder is brilliant for grinding nuts really finely for making flour, if you do not have a food processor. They are cheap and can be found in almost any kitchen equipment store.

DEHYDRATOR
A dehydrator is a type of oven which dries foods at temperatures below 42°C. In this way you can prepare delicious and crisp food without using an oven. It is also one of the oldest ways of conserving food. In this book I only use the dehydrator for making cookies. But if you do not have a dehydrator, do not despair. You can easily make the cookies anyway and the recipes are also delicious with all their juiciness intact.

GRATER

A grater is used for grating everything from carrots to the zest of citrus fruits. Many food processors also have a raw food function but I prefer an old fashioned grater. Citrus peel, ginger and spices should be grated ' julienne' style – that means finely.

ICE MAKER

I use the ice maker when making 'ice cream', i.e. based on nut milk. An ice maker is not an absolute must for making ice cream, but it makes it much better and the consistency is like real bought ice cream, since the ice crystals are destroyed during freezing which give the ice cream a softer structure.

SPRING FORMS, CAKE TINS AND CUTTERS

I love cake tins and use them for most of my cakes. Cake tins are available in many different shapes and sizes and if you are serious about cake making you should go on a discovery journey in the world of cake tins.

SPRING FORMS

I always use spring forms for the soft cream cakes. The cakes will keep their shape better when the sides of the tin are removable. You can line the bottom with baking paper before tightening the sides. This makes it much easier to remove the finished cake from the tin.

TART DISHES

I always recommend tart dishes with a removable base. If you don't have one you could line your tart dish with cling film which makes it easier to take the tart base out of the dish.

BROWNIE TINS/RECTANGULAR TINS

I prefer to use a brownie tin or a rectangular tin for brownies. But you could also use an ordinary oven proof dish or shape them by hand.

MUFFIN SHEETS

Used for cupcakes. It is a sort of baking sheet with hollows for muffins, perfect for the soft cup cake pastry. Remember to line the hollows with paper cupcake liners.

CUTTERS

Cutters are available in all shapes and sizes from stars and hearts to Christmas trees and pigs. I use them for cookies and for fruit. You could for example cut a mango, watermelon or pineapple in thin slices and cut them into colourful hearts and stars. This will make beautiful decorations for any type of cake.

Magic and alchemy
— about the magical ingredients

Some of the cakes contain ingredients which may seem different and exotic compared to ordinary cake recipes. Some of these I use instead of traditional 'cake ingredients', for example natural sweeteners such as birch sugar instead of sugar, raw cocoa instead of roasted cocoa and coconut oil instead of butter. Other ingredients I will use to give more colour or an exotic flavour and others to increase the nutritional contents. Many of the ingredients may almost be considered food supplements. Super foods are – as the name indicates – foods with almost supernatural powers. They contain many nutrients, not least antioxidants and other plant chemicals. Remember also our own domestic super foods, the fresh berries and fruits. I always buy organic produce whenever possible. The minimum requirement you ought to demand from your food is to avoid putting poison on it.

AGAVE SYRUP
Agave syrup is derived from the agave cactus which is also used for making tequila. Agave syrup affects the blood sugar less than sugar, since it has a relatively low glycaemic index (approx.34). In the recipes I mainly use agave syrup, but you can use your own favourite sweetener.

BIRCH SUGAR
Birch sugar consists of the sugar alcohol xylitol, which is naturally present in birch trees. Birch sugar is very like sugar but has a very low glycaemic index (approx.8) which means that it has almost no effect on the blood sugar. Birch sugar is also found to have a beneficial effect for the prevention of caries in teeth. However birch sugar is not easily soluble in cakes and can give a slightly crispy texture.

BLUE MANNA
Blue manna is an extract of an algae (Aphanizomenon flos aquae) that contains large quantities of phycocyanin, a blue pigment with antioxidant effect. The algae also contains large quantities of phenylethylamine, which is also found in chocolate, a substance which helps concentration and attention and which gives a feeling of pleasure and well being. Since blue manna is a blue dye I often use it for icing. It gives a brilliant, blue colour. But be careful not to put too much in, since blue manna in large quantities tastes of algae.

CHIA SEEDS
Chia seeds also called Salba are small seeds rich in Omega 3 fatty acids and fibre. Gram for gram chia seeds contain eight times more Omega 3 than salmon, four times more fibre than flax, six times more calcium than milk, 30% more antioxidants than blueberries and fifteen times more magnesium than broccoli. Vegans are very concerned about getting 'real' protein every day. Chia seeds are a complete protein supplement and contain all eight essential amino acids (i.e. the ones the body cannot produce and there-fore must have from the diet). Chia seeds give a total protein supplement of 21% per 100g. Chia

seeds also absorb fluid and like psyllium seed husks can also be used as a binding agent in the recipes.

CHLORELLA

Chlorella is a green algae and a fantastic source of protein since chlorella like chia seeds is a complete protein supplement with all eight essential amino acids, vitamins (e.g. B12), minerals and chlorophyll, and it can also bind heavy metals and excrete them from the body. Chlorella has an intensive deep green colour and is a brilliant dye. Mix it with your icing for cup cakes for a brilliant green colour. You can also use chlorella mixed with a little agave syrup and shredded coconut for making green sprinkles for ice cream and cakes.

GOJI BERRIES

Goji berries have for thousands of years been used in traditional Chinese medicine. The berry is packed with antioxidants. The taste is like a mixture between raisins and cranberries. Goji berry is also a complete protein supplement and contains up to 21 trace minerals that are important for all the chemical processes in the body. It is the most important source of carotene and contains more than 500 times the amount of vitamin C found in oranges. Goji berry also contains polysaccharides which strengthen the immune system.

HEMP SEEDS

Hemp seeds taste wonderful and a little like nuts! You can increase the nutritional value of cakes by adding hemp seeds to the cake base. Hemp seeds constitute a complete protein source containing all eight essential amino acids. Hemp seeds are made up of 65% edestin which can be absorbed by the body in its raw state, in contrast to the protein found in soya beans which has to be either cooked or sprouted. Hemp seeds contain no THC, the psychoactive substance found in hash.

HEMP OIL

Hemp oil is used as a food supplement due to its content of all the essential fatty acids (i.e. both Omega 3 and 6) and it will therefore cover the daily requirement. Hemp oil contains 57% linoleic acid also known as Omega 6 and 19% linolenic acid also known as Omega 3. Hemp oil is also a good source of fatty acid, GLA which is thought to remedy premenstrual tension.

PSYLLIUM SEED HUSKS

I use psyllium seed husks as a binding agent in several of the recipes. They have a great capacity for absorption and at the same time add fibre which will contribute to maintaining a stable blood sugar level. If you have put too much liquid in a recipe, a few psyllium seed husks will often save the cake.

FLAX SEED OIL

The fat content of flax seed oil consists of 55% of the unsaturated Omega 3 fatty acid called alpha linolenic acid or ALA. This is an essential fatty acid which the body can convert to a group of substances with hormone-like effect known as prostaglandins, which regulate many bodily functions including the immune system, blood platelet activity and blood pressure. Flax seed oil keeps you subtle, makes your skin soft and remedies hormonal imbalances.

INCA BERRIES

Inca berries are also known as Cape gooseberry or physalis. They are acidic and juicy and packed with nutrients. Inca berries are known as a good source of vitamin P (bioflavonoids) and are rich in the plant fibre pectin which amongst others has a cholesterol lowering effect and at the same time may stabilize the blood sugar level. They have a high content of phosphorus, vitamin A,C, B1, B2, B6 and B12. They also have a high protein content for a fruit (16%).

COCOA BUTTER

Cocoa butter is the fat extracted from cocoa beans (approx. 40-50% of the bean).Cocoa butter has a very mild cocoa taste and is used in the production of chocolate. Cocoa butter has a melting point around 34-38°C. Therefore chocolate is solid at room temperature but melts when you put it in your mouth. I often use cocoa butter to keep the shape of the cakes in order to stop them melting at room temperature. Cocoa butter contains natural antioxidants which keep your skin beautiful and at the same time stops the butter going rancid. Therefore cocoa butter will keep for up to 4-5 years. As cocoa butter is solid at room temperature it should be gently melted over a bain marie or on top of the radiator before use. Cocoa butter can also be grated finely using a grater.

COCONUT OIL

Coconut oil is, like cocoa butter, solid at room temperature and is therefore also used to keep the shape of cakes. Coconut oil contains a fatty acid called lauric acid known for its antiviral, antibacterial and fungicidal effect. This fatty acid has been shown to increase digestion, reduce the risk of cardiovascular diseases and high blood pressure. In order to form steroid hormones the body needs saturated fat and this is when coconut oil is a fantastic building block, especially in the formation of the female sex hormone progesterone and the male sex hormone testosterone. In my clinic I see more and more men and women who produce too little of these hormones. Progesterone and testosterone also help to increase the formation of neurotransmitters such as dopamine and serotonin which contribute to the feeling of well being.

LECITHIN GRANULES

Lecithin granules have a lovely creamy taste and make it possible to make 'cream cakes' which both lower the cholesterol and improve memory. Lecithin granules are used as a food supplement, a fatty acid which contains a phospholipid which is an important part of our neurotransmitters. It improves memory and at the same time controls cholesterol. Lecithin is an important part of the membranes in our cell walls. Lecithin is extracted typically from soya beans or sunflower seeds. If you use soya lecithin take care to use a GM free product.

LUCUMA POWDER

Lucuma is a fruit from South America also known as the 'Gold of the Incas'. It tastes a little like maple syrup, caramel or malt and at the same time a little dusty. Lucuma powder absorbs liquid so if you add lucuma powder to the recipes, you should add the same quantity of liquid. Lucuma is a great source of carbohydrates, food fibres, vitamins and minerals. It is packed with beta-carotene, niacine (B3) and iron.

MACA

Maca is a root from Peru. Its Latin name is Lepidium meynii but it is also known as 'the Ginseng of Peru' or 'the Ginseng of the Amazon'. The taste is a little special, but can be hidden in chocolate cakes, e.g. you can use it to good effect in brownies. Maca is packed with vitamins, minerals, enzymes and is a complete protein supplement. It is also a so-called adaptogen herb which contributes to increasing the body's resistance to stress and infections. Maca can be used as a strengthening and hormone regulating supplement for PMT, climacteric problems, deficiency of testosterone and as an aphrodisiac.

MULBERRY

Mulberry has a crisp, sweet almost caramel taste and is full of nutrition. It has been used for many years in Chinese medicine. Each berry is packed with nutrition, in particular iron, calcium, fibre and vitamin C and K. It is also rich in antioxidants, in particular resveratrol. Resveratrol is a natural antibiotic which is used by the plants to fight infection and bacteria and fungal attacks.

STEVIA

Stevia is a natural sweetener extracted from the South American herb Stevia rebaudiana and which in its most concentrated form is approx. 300 times sweeter than ordinary processed sugar. So be careful when using it and try it before adding it to cakes. Stevia is available in a green, a white (stevioside) and in liquid form. Stevia has been known for centuries for its healing properties and the latest research now indicates that Stevia can have a beneficial use in the treatment of type 2 diabetes. If you are diabetic I would recommend that you use Stevia as a sweetener.

RAW HONEY

Raw or honey that has not been heat treated can also be used as a sweetener. Raw honey is very light and forms small crystals. It is precisely these crystals that indicate that the honey has not been heat treated and has preserved its enzyme activity – and all its nutrients. Raw honey contains an enzyme which predigests the sugars in the honey. The honey you find in supermarkets has been heat treated. Raw honey contains many antioxidants, strengthens the immune system and has antibacterial properties.

RAW COCOA

The Latin name of cocoa is Theobroma kakao which means the food of the Gods. When I use cocoa it is always raw cocoa. Raw cocoa is sold as whole beans, as nibs (pieces of beans) and as a powder. Raw cocoa is not roasted like ordinary cocoa powder and in this way many of its fantastic properties will be retained which would otherwise be destroyed by roasting. Cocoa contains an incredible amount of minerals, and it scores top points for antioxidant values. Raw cocoa also contains substances such as theobromine, a plant chemical related to caffeine and phenyle-thylamine which is known for giving a feeling of happiness and excitement and which increases concentration. Finally cocoa contains great quantities of magnesium which means it can be used as a muscle relaxing agent. But avoid having cocoa before bedtime, for although the muscles will relax, cocoa is also very stimulating!

Final word of advice

You will need a freezer and/or a fridge to chill the cakes to make them set and enable you to remove the sides of the cake tins. This is especially important for the cream cakes in the first section.

I always recommend that you soak nuts and seeds before use. It makes them more easily digestible and at the same time the nutrients are released and the sprouting process is brought to life.

Nuts used for cream or ice cream should also be soaked before use to achieve the desired consistency. Therefore the soaking time is always indicated with the recipes.

Cashew nuts can be hard for the digestive system. In all the recipes where cashew nuts are used, you can use macamadia nuts instead.

Natural ingredients can vary enormously in their content of liquid and sweetness. Therefore always make sure to taste the desserts throughout the preparation to ensure the best possible result.

EAT LIKE YOU
GIVE A DAMN

Cakes

Of course I can have my cake and eat it too!

16 cm

Blueberry Dream

A purple dream of a cream cake both fresh and sweet.

Serves approx. 8–10 people

CAKE BASE
120g Brazil nuts
85g dates, stones removed
2 tbsp coconut oil
1 tsp vanilla powder
20g mulberries, coarsely chopped

BLUEBERRY CREAM
350g cashew nuts, soaked in water for approx.
  2 hours
100 ml agave syrup
2 tbsp lecithin granules
4 tbsp coconut oil
1 tbsp cocoa butter
125g blueberries, fresh or frozen (frozen
  berries should be defrosted and any liquid
  poured away)
2 tsp psyllium seed husks or finely ground
  chia seeds

DECORATION
'Whipped cream' (see page 141)
Fresh blueberries

Cake base: Chop the Brazil nuts finely or grind them finely in a coffee grinder. Blend dates, coconut oil and vanilla powder to a smooth paste. Mix well with the ground nuts and mulberries. Line a spring form with baking paper and arrange the pastry in the base of the spring form.

Blueberry cream: Blend the cashew nuts with agave syrup, lecithin granules, coconut oil and cocoa butter to a fine cream without lumps or visible pieces of cashew nuts. Add blueberries and blend again. Finally add the chia seeds or psyllium seed husks and blend for the last time. Pour the cream over the base and place the cake in the freezer for approx. 1 hour, before removing the sides of the spring form and the baking paper. Decorate with 'whipped cream' and fresh blueberries.

BLUEBERRIES have for centuries been used medicinally due to their healing properties. They contain ellagic acid, a powerful antioxidant that protects our cells. Blueberries contain anthocyanins which strengthen the capillaries and improves circulation. They are also thought to improve sight, counteract dementia and cardiovascular diseases. They contain anti-inflammatory salicylates and tannin, which can fight the bacteria that cause cystitis.

Banana Chocolate Cake

This cake is a real festive treat and who wouldn't like the divine combination of banana and chocolate.

Serves approx. 8–10 people

CAKE BASE
120g mixed walnuts and Brazil nuts
10 dates, stones removed

VANILLA CREAM
175g cashew nuts, soaked in water for 2 hours
50 ml agave syrup
1 tbsp lemon juice
1 tbsp coconut oil
½ tsp vanilla powder
A little water

CHOCOLATE SAUCE
2 medium bananas
2 tbsp raisins, previously soaked
10 dates, stones removed
2 tbsp raw cocoa
½ tsp vanilla powder
1 tbsp coconut oil
1 tsp cocoa butter

DECORATION AND FILLING
1 banana cut into slices
30g Brazil nuts and pecan nuts
  coarsely chopped

Cake base: Chop the walnuts and the Brazil nuts finely or grind them finely in a coffee grinder. Blend the dates to a purée, add a little water or coconut oil, if necessary, to make the blender work. Mix the ground nuts and date purée to a paste and add to the base of a spring form lined with baking paper. Leave to cool in the fridge.

Vanilla cream: Blend the cashew nuts with agave syrup, lemon juice, coconut oil, vanilla powder and a little water, if necessary, to make the blender turn. Blend to a thick vanilla cream.

Chocolate sauce: Make a thick chocolate sauce by blending the two bananas with the pre-soaked raisins, dates, raw cocoa, vanilla powder, coconut oil and cocoa butter.

Decoration and filling: Cover the base of the spring form with the vanilla cream. Then pour half of the chocolate filling over and sprinkle chopped nuts and slices of banana over the whole cake. Finally spread the remaining chocolate sauce over the cake and freeze for approx. 1 hour, before removing the spring form. Decorate with a couple of slices of banana or a little fresh fruit.

BANANAS contain B5 which strengthens your immune system and B6 which strengthens the body's ability to detoxify. Bananas are also rich in the amino acid tryptophan which the body converts to serotonin, a signal substance which makes the body relax.

Mango Cheesecake

A fresh and tropical mango cream over a soft layer of 'cheesy cream' on a crisp and sweet base.

Serves approx. 8–10 people

CAKE BASE
60g almonds
85g dates, stones removed
2 tbsp coconut oil
1 tsp vanilla powder
50 ml mulberries

CHEESY CREAM
350g cashew nuts, soaked in water for 2 hours
100 ml agave syrup
5 tbsp lemon juice
1 tsp vanilla powder
4 tbsp coconut oil
1 tsp cocoa butter
½ tsp Himalayan salt
A little water, if necessary

MANGO PURÉE
150g fresh mango cut into slices
30g dried mango, soaked in water for approx. 2 hours
1 very ripe banana
1 tbsp coconut oil
2 tsp finely ground chia seeds or psyllium seed husks
If necessary add ½ tsp turmeric if you want a more intensive yellow colour

Cake base: Grind the almonds finely in a powerful blender or coffee grinder. Blend the finely ground almonds with dates, coconut oil and vanilla powder and then mix in the mulberries. Place the pastry in a spring form lined with baking paper and leave in the fridge while preparing the cheesy cream.

Cheesy cream: Blend the cashew nuts with agave syrup, lemon juice, vanilla powder, coconut oil, cocoa butter and Himalayan salt in a blender, add a little water to make sure the ingredients will be well mixed. Pour the cream over the base of the spring form and chill the cake in the freezer while you prepare the mango purée.

Mango purée: Blend fresh and dried mango with a banana, coconut oil, chia seeds or psyllium seed husks and pour over the cake which is now set. Chill the cake in the freezer. After approx. 1 hour in the freezer the cake is set and you can remove the sides of the spring form and the baking paper. Serve with fresh fruit.

MANGO is packed with beta-carotene which the body converts to the virus fighting vitamin A. The mango is also rich in vitamin C which makes your skin firm and at the same time regulates our immune system. Mango is also one of the only fruits which contain the antioxidant vitamin E. Mango has antibacterial, antiviral and antiseptic properties.

16 cm

Chocolate Cream Cake with Strawberry Mousse

A light and yet filling mousse cake made with avocado.

Serves approx. 8–10 people

CAKE BASE
15 dates, stones removed
3 tbsp coconut oil
1 tsp cocoa butter
1 pinch of Himalayan salt
60g Brazil nuts
50g shredded coconut
2 tbsp raw cocoa powder

CHOCOLATE CREAM
1 large, ripe avocado
50 ml agave syrup or honey
3 tbsp cocoa butter
100 ml coconut oil
100 ml raw cocoa
10 dates soaked in water
4 tbsp lecithin granules
1 pinch Himalayan salt
2 tsp finely ground chia seeds or Psyllium
    seed husks

STRAWBERRY MOUSSE
60g cashew nuts, soaked in water for 1-2
    hours
1 tbsp coconut oil
50 ml agave syrup
100 ml fresh or frozen (defrosted)
    strawberries
2 tbsp lecithin granules
2 tbsp psyllium seed husks

DECORATION
Fresh strawberries cut in halves

Cake base: Blend dates and coconut oil, cocoa butter and Himalayan salt to a paste. Grind the Brazil nuts in a coffee grinder or chop them finely and mix with shredded coconut and cocoa powder with the date paste. Line the base of the spring form with baking paper before 'tightening' the sides. This way it will be easier to remove the cakes from the spring form before serving. Press the pastry flat into a spring form and place the halved strawberries in a row along the edge of the spring form. Leave to chill in the fridge.

Chocolate cream: Blend avocado, agave syrup, cocoa butter and coconut oil. Then add dates and finally raw cocoa, lecithin granules, salt and chia seeds. Blend to a cream and add a little water, if necessary, to make the chocolate cream a little more smooth. Pour the chocolate cream into the spring form and take care the strawberries do not topple over. Leave to chill again, in the freezer, if possible.

Strawberry mousse: Blend cashew nuts, coconut oil, agave syrup, strawberries, lecithin granules and psyllium seed husks to a creamy and pink mousse and pour into an icing bag. Decorate the cake with small dots of pink mousse. When the cake has chilled and is completely set, you can open the spring form. Remove the baking paper and leave the cake on a serving dish – decorate with fresh berries.

20 cm

Lemon Full Moon

A lovely fresh and not too rich cake – perfect for warm summer days with lots of fresh fruit. You can also make the filling without the cake base and serve it as a healthy version of lemon mousse. Add a little extra liquid, e.g. almond milk to get a lighter lemon mousse.

Serves approx. 12 people

CAKE BASE
125g almonds, soaked in water for approx. 2 hours
85g dates, stones removed
1 tbsp coconut oil
25g shredded coconut

LEMON CREAM
350g cashew nuts, soaked in water for 2 hours
4 tbsp coconut oil
1 tbsp cocoa butter, grated or melted
5 tbsp lemon juice
3 tbsp raw honey
1 tsp vanilla powder
1 tsp grated lemon zest
1 tsp turmeric (for colour)
2 tbsp lecithin granules
1 pinch salt

DECORATION
'Whipped Cream' (see page 141) and fresh berries

Cake base: Chop the almonds finely or grind them in a coffee grinder. Blend dates and coconut oil and then add the chopped/ground almonds and the shredded coconut. Spread the paste over the base of a spring form lined with baking paper. Leave to chill while you prepare the lemon cream.

Lemon cream: Blend cashew nuts with coconut oil, cocoa butter, lemon juice and honey in a powerful blender. Add vanilla powder, lemon zest, turmeric, lecithin granules and salt and blend again until you have a thick, pale yellow cream.

Pour the lemon cream into the spring form and leave the cake in the freezer for a minimum of an hour until set and the sides of the spring form can be removed. Serve with 'whipped cream' and fresh berries.

LEMONS are packed with vitamin C, folic acid (vitamin B), potassium and sodium and precisely due to their high content of potassium and sodium freshly squeezed lemonade is the perfect isotonic drink after training. The high vitamin C content also makes lemons a good remedy for infections and strengthens the immune system. Lemons contain a substance called limonene which gives them their characteristic citrus flavour.

20 cm

Kïnky Pïnky

A very lady like cake, which is also perfect for princess birthday parties.

Serves approx. 12 people

CAKE BASE
85g dates, stones removed
1 tbsp flax seed oil
1 tsp vanilla powder
2 tbsp Brazil nuts
100g shredded coconut
45g dried mulberries, coarsely chopped

RASPBERRY CREAM
350g cashew nuts, soaked in water for approx.
  2 hours
100 ml agave syrup
200g raspberries, fresh or frozen
4 tbsp coconut oil
2 tbsp cocoa butter

COCONUT DECORATION
35g blueberries
3 tbsp agave syrup
100g shredded coconut

Cake base: Blend dates, flax seed oil and vanilla powder to a smooth paste. Add Brazil nuts and shredded coconut using a powerful blender or food processor. Turn the pastry into a bowl and mix in the chopped mulberries. Line a spring form with baking paper and spread the pastry over the base of the spring form.

Raspberry cream: Blend the cashew nuts with agave syrup and raspberries to a very fine cream without lumps or visible pieces of cashew nuts. Then add coconut oil and cocoa butter and blend again. Pour the cream over the base and leave the cake in the freezer for approx. 1 hour.

Coconut decoration: Blend blueberries with agave syrup and pour the blueberry syrup into a bowl. Thoroughly mix it with the shredded coconut. When the cake is completely set, using a sharp knife cut around the sides and remove the spring form. Remove the baking paper and serve the cake on a cake dish. Before serving decorate the sides with the purple coconut sprinkles.

White Chocolate Cheesecake with Raspberries

At least as delicious and 'naughty' as the old fashioned version.

Serves approx. 8–10 people

CAKE BASE
60g Brazil nuts
40g dates, stones removed
1 tsp coconut oil
25g shredded coconut

CHEESY CREAM
300g cashew nuts soaked in water
    for at least 1 hour
50 ml water
50 ml lemon juice
50 ml agave syrup
100 ml coconut oil
40g cocoa butter
1 tsp vanilla powder
¾ tsp Himalayan salt

RASPBERRY PURÉE
200g fresh or frozen raspberries
3 tbsp agave syrup
2 tsp finely ground chia seeds or psyllium
    seed husks

Cake base: Chop the nuts coarsely. Then blend the dates with the coconut oil, adding a little water, if necessary. Mix the date paste, chopped nuts and shredded coconut to a paste. Line the base of a spring form with baking paper which makes it easier to remove the finished cake from the form. Place the paste in the spring form and leave to chill while preparing the cheesy cream and the raspberry purée.

Cheesy cream: Blend cashew nuts with water. Add lemon juice, agave syrup, coconut oil, cocoa butter, vanilla powder and Himalayan salt and blend. Pour the cream over the nut base in the spring form and leave to chill (fridge or freezer).

Raspberry purée: Make the raspberry purée by blending raspberries, agave syrup and 2 tsp finely ground chia seeds or psyllium seed husks. Pour the purée over the cooled and set cheesecake. When the cake is set, remove the sides of the spring form and decorate the cake with fresh fruit.

RASPBERRIES are one of the fruits which contain the most food fibre which contributes to keeping low cholesterol and maintaining a healthy digestion. Raspberries have a high vitamin C content and are rich in the antioxidant group anthocyanins. They also contain B3, folate, biotin and iron.

Carrot Cake

Rabbit food in the delicious way!

Serves approx. 6 people

CARROT CAKE
250g finely grated carrot
125g almonds, soaked in water for 2 hours
125g dates, stones removed
1 tsp nutmeg
1 tsp ground cinnamon
1 tbsp finely grated ginger
1 tbsp grated orange zest
1 tbsp grated lemon zest
90g walnuts, soaked in water for 2 hours,
    coarsely chopped
65g raisins

'CREAM CHEESE' ICING
115g macadamia nuts, soaked in water for
    2 hours
1 tbsp lemon juice
1 tbsp agave syrup
1 pinch Himalayan salt
1 tsp vanilla powder
A little water

Carrot cake: Grate the carrots very finely. Grind the almonds in a powerful blender or food processor and add the dates. Pour the paste into a bowl and add the grated carrots, spices, orange and lemon zest. Add the chopped walnuts and raisins. Shape the cake as you wish, e.g. in a small baking tray.

'Cream cheese' icing: Blend macadamia nuts, lemon juice, agave syrup, Himalayan salt and vanilla powder with a little water in a powerful blender. Add a little water, if necessary to make it a little lighter to mix. Spread the 'cream cheese' icing over the finished carrot cake just before serving.

CARROTS It is said that carrots are good for the eyes – they contain beta-carotene the precursor to vitamin A. Lack of vitamin A may cause deterioration of sight, especially the capacity to see in the dark. Carrots are rich in vitamin K which counteracts bruising – and they contain many food fibres good for the heart and digestion. Carrots are rich in chrome which helps to stabilise the blood sugar.

20 cm

After Eight Cake

A delicious mixture of chocolate and mint – definitely also before 8 pm.

Serves approx. 12 people

CAKE BASE
250g dates, stones removed
1 tbsp cocoa butter
1 tbsp coconut oil
3 tbsp agave syrup
2 tsp vanilla powder
5 tbsp raw cocoa powder
1 pinch salt
60g Brazil nuts, soaked in water for 2 hours
 T and coarsely chopped

MINT CREAM
350g cashew nuts, soaked in water for 2 hours
100 ml almond milk (see page 135, can
   be replaced by water and 1 tsp extra
   lecithin granules)
1 tbsp cocoa butter
4 tbsp coconut oil
7 tbsp agave syrup
2 tbsp lecithin granules
3g squeezed mint leaves
3 drops peppermint oil

Cake base: Blend dates, cocoa butter, coconut oil and agave syrup and add vanilla powder, cocoa powder, salt and nuts. Spread the paste over the base of a spring form lined with baking paper and leave to chill.

Mint cream: Blend cashew nuts with almond milk, cocoa butter, coconut oil, agave syrup and lecithin granules to a soft cream. Then add the mint leaves and mint oil and blend thoroughly. Pour the mint cream into the spring form and leave the cake in the freezer for at least 1 hour until the cake is set, and then remove the sides of the spring form and the baking paper. Decorate with fresh mint leaves before serving.

PEPPERMINT has for centuries been used against stomach problems and nausea, influenza and colds and it stimulates circulation. In unison cocoa and mint have a good synergy – the substance menthol in the mint expands the capillaries so the cocoa's properties more easily reach your cells! Cocoa has a high content of magnesium which is necessary for absorbing calcium from the mint.

Oreo Cake

Soft vanilla cream surrounded by crisp chocolate cake crumble – it will certainly become a hit when you serve this cake for your guests.

Serves approx. 8–10 people

CAKE BASE (AND TOP)
115g Brazil nuts
125g almonds
165g dates, stones removed
50 ml coconut oil
2 tbsp cocoa butter
3 tbsp agave syrup
5 tbsp cocoa powder
45g mulberries, coarsely chopped

VANILLA CREAM
350g cashew nuts, soaked in water for approx. 2 hours
200 ml almond milk (see page 135, can be replaced by water and 2 tsp lecithin granules, if necessary)
100 ml coconut oil
1 tbsp cocoa butter
100 ml agave syrup
4 tsp vanilla powder
5 tbsp lecithin granules

Cake base (and top): Finely grind Brazil nuts and almonds. Blend dates, coconut oil, cocoa butter and agave syrup to a smooth paste. Add the chopped nuts and cocoa powder and finally fold the chopped mulberries into the paste. Divide the paste into two equal portions. Place one portion over the base of the spring form lined with baking paper and then loosen it carefully. Place on a dish or board and keep chilled. Now place the second portion over the base of the spring form and leave to chill, while you prepare the vanilla cream.

Vanilla cream: Blend cashew nuts with almond milk, coconut oil, cocoa butter, agave syrup, vanilla powder and lecithin granules. Pour the vanilla cream into the spring form and leave the cake in the freezer for at least 1 hour until completely set. Place the other 'cake base' at the top of the spring form and remove the sides of the spring form and the baking paper.

COCOA AND VANILLA

have a fantastic synergy. Vanilla comes from the vanilla orchid which can grow on the cocoa tree, a matching pair from nature. In fact according to ancient mythology cocoa and vanilla were gods who fell in love and took the shape on earth as plants. Vanilla is considered an aphrodisiac and is also calming and seductive.

20 cm

Forest Berry Cream Cake

A real late summer cake packed with small antioxidant bombs.

Serves approx. 12 people

CAKE BASE
90g pecan nuts
90g walnuts
85g dates, stones removed
1 tbsp coconut oil

FOREST BERRY CREAM
350g cashew nuts, soaked in water for 2 hours
100 ml almond milk (see page 135, can be replaced by water and a little extra lecithin granules)
4 tbsp coconut oil
1 tbsp cocoa butter
50 ml agave syrup or raw honey
1 tsp vanilla powder
2 tbsp lecithin granules
2 tsp finely ground chia seeds or psyllium seed husks
60g mixed berries (to be blended with the cream) + 120g mixed fresh berries (for example blackberries, raspberries, blueberries and strawberries)

Cake base: Grind pecan nuts and walnuts in a blender or coffee grinder. Blend dates and coconut oil to a paste and mix in the nuts. Spread over the base of a spring form, lined with baking paper and leave to chill while you prepare the forest berry cream.

Forest berry cream: Blend cashew nuts with almond milk and add coconut oil, cocoa butter, agave syrup, vanilla powder, lecithin granules and finely ground chia seeds or psyllium seed husks. Blend the cream with 100 ml mixed berries. Pour the cream into a bowl and carefully fold in the rest of the fresh berries. Spread the berry cream in the spring form and place in the freezer for approx. 1 hour or until it is completely set and the sides of the spring form can be removed.

BERRIES Many people believe that berries belong to the healthiest of all foods. So healthy are they that a multitude of illnesses in many cases can be prevented if you eat a good portion of berries every day. That is simply due to the unique combination of valuable vitamins, minerals and plant substances.

16 cm

Caramel Cake

Chocolate base, peanut butter cream filling topped with caramel sauce – need I say more?

Serves approx. 8–10 people

CAKE BASE
120g Brazil nuts
85g dates, stones removed
2 tbsp agave syrup
2 tbsp coconut oil
45g mulberries, coarsely chopped
3 tbsp raw cocoa powder

PEANUT BUTTER CREAM
300g cashew nuts, soaked for approx. 2 hours
4 tbsp coconut oil
2 tbsp cocoa butter
100 ml agave syrup
60g raw Jungle Peanuts, soaked in water for at
   least 2 hours
2 tbsp lecithin granules
2 tbsp finely ground chia seeds or psyllium
   seed husks

CARAMEL TOPPING
100 ml caramel sauce (see page 136)
2 tsp lucuma powder

Cake base: Grind Brazil nuts in a blender or coffee grinder. Blend dates, agave syrup and coconut oil to a smooth paste. Pour the date paste into a bowl and mix in the rest of the ingredients. Spread the paste over the base of a spring form lined with baking paper. Leave the base to chill.

Peanut butter cream: Blend cashew nuts, coconut oil, cocoa butter, agave syrup, Jungle Peanuts, lecithin granules and the finely ground chia seeds or psyllium seed husks to a creamy consistency, free of lumps from the nuts. Pour the peanut butter cream into the spring form and place the cake in the freezer for approx. 1 hour, until it is so firmly set that you are able to open the spring form and remove the baking paper.

Caramel topping: Mix the caramel sauce with lucuma powder and stir it well. Pour over the cake and serve with berries and fresh fruit.

JUNGLE PEANUTS are wild, raw peanuts. They contain 26% protein, which is more than any other nut. Over 40% of the oils in this nut consist of simple unsaturated Omega 9 which is considered to be good for the heart and circulation. Jungle Peanuts also contain all eight essential amino acids, i.e. a fully comprehensive protein.

Coconut Cream Cakes

As pretty as tiny snow clad ice bergs

Serves approx. 4–5 people

CAKE BASES
165g dates, stones removed
1 pinch sea salt
1 tbsp coconut oil
140g shredded coconut

COCONUT CREAM
120g cashew nuts
200 ml coconut milk (see page 135)
1 ripe banana
4 tbsp coconut oil
1 tbsp cocoa butter
2 tbsp agave syrup
1 tsp vanilla powder
3 tbsp lecithin granules
2 tsp finely ground chia seeds or psyllium
    seed husks

DECORATION
Coconut flakes

Cake base: Blend dates, salt and coconut oil. Add shredded coconut. Place the paste between two pieces of baking paper and roll out to a thickness of approx. 1 cm. The baking paper stops the paste from sticking. Cut out small circles with the bowls. Place the bases on a tray and leave to chill while you prepare the coconut cream.

Coconut cream: Leave the cashew nuts to soak for approx. 1 hour in the homemade coconut milk. Blend coconut milk, cashew nuts, banana, coconut oil, cocoa butter, agave syrup, vanilla powder and lecithin granules. Finally blend with chia seeds or psyllium seed husks.

Line the bowls with cling film or use the tart dishes and pour the coconut cream into the forms. Place the bowls in the freezer for approx. 1 hour until the cream is set, then remove from the bowls. Place the cream tops on top of the bases and decorate with coconut flakes.

COCONUT has for thousands of years been highly treasured and in traditional medicine all over the world it has been used for the treatment of a number of health problems, including boils, asthma, bronchitis, ear ache, head lice and many more. Like mother's milk, coconut contains lauric acid which fights viruses, bacteria and fungal diseases

16 cm

Banana Berry Cake

A summery and pretty cake – fresh and light.

Serves approx. 8–10 people

CAKE BASE
85g dates, stones removed
50g shredded coconut
60g coarsely chopped Brazil nuts

BANANA CREAM
120g cashew nuts, soaked in water for approx.
  2 hours
2 ripe bananas
3 tbsp coconut oil
1 tbsp cocoa butter
50 ml agave syrup
1 tsp vanilla powder
2 tsp finely ground chia seeds or psyllium
  seed husks

DECORATION
Fresh blackberries, blueberries, raspberries
  and strawberries

Cake base: Blend dates, adding a little water, if necessary, to a smooth paste and then mix in shredded coconut and the chopped nuts. Place the paste in a spring form lined with baking paper and leave to chill in the freezer while you prepare the banana cream.

Banana cream: Blend cashew nuts, bananas, coconut oil, cocoa butter, agave syrup, vanilla powder and finely ground chia seeds or psyllium seed husks. Pour the banana cream into the spring form and leave in the freezer for approx. 1 hour until the cake is set and you are able to open the spring form and remove the baking paper.

Decorate with the fresh berries.

16 cm

Ganache à trois

A delicious raw chocolate cake with three different kinds of chocolate. Almost too much of a good thing – but only just.

Serves approx. 8–10 people

CHOCOLATE BASE
60g Brazil nuts
165g dates, stones removed
1 tbsp cocoa butter
1 tbsp coconut oil
2 tbsp agave syrup
50g shredded coconut
3 tbsp raw cocoa powder
60g raw cocoa nibs

GANACHE
200 ml almond milk to mix it thoroughly (see page 135, can be replaced by water)
120g cashew nuts, soaked in water for 2 hours
3 tbsp coconut oil
3 tbsp lecithin granules
4 tbsp agave syrup
165g dates, stones removed
3 tbsp raw cocoa powder
1 tsp vanilla powder
3 tbsp lucuma powder

CHOCOLATE ICING
3 tbsp raw cocoa powder
2 tbsp coconut oil
2 tbsp cocoa butter
2 tbsp agave syrup

DECORATION
Goji berries or other super food berries and fresh fruit

Cake base: Chop the Brazil nuts coarsely. Blend dates with cocoa butter, coconut oil and agave syrup and then mix in shredded coconut, raw cocoa powder, cocoa nibs and nuts. Fill the base of a spring form lined with baking paper and leave to chill while you prepare the ganache.

Ganache: Blend almond milk with cashew nuts, coconut oil, lecithin granules and agave syrup. When you have a thick cream add dates, cocoa powder, vanilla and lucuma powder and blend well.

Pour the ganache over the base and leave to chill for a minimum 1 hour, until the cake is completely set, when you can remove the sides and the baking paper. Meanwhile prepare the chocolate icing.

Chocolate icing: Blend raw cocoa powder, coconut oil, cocoa butter and agave syrup and coat the cold cake with the mixture.

Serve with goji berries or other super fruits and lots of fresh fruit.

16 cm

Piña Colada Cream Cake

Pineapple and coconut together in a lovely union – just add calypso rhythms and a raffia skirt.

Serves approx. 8–10 people

CAKE BASE
85g dates, stones removed
1 tsp coconut oil
100g shredded coconut

CREAM
350g cashew nuts, soaked in water for 2 hours
100 ml agave syrup
1 tsp vanilla powder
4 tbsp coconut oil
1 tbsp cocoa butter
A little water, if necessary

PINEAPPLE PURÉE
80g pineapple
50g dried pineapple, soaked in water
1 ripe banana
1 tbsp coconut oil
2 tbsp psyllium seed husks

DECORATION
'Whipped Cream' (see page 141)
2 tbsp shredded coconut mixed with 2 tbsp
  chopped dried pineapple

Cake base: Blend the dates to a smooth paste with the coconut oil and then mix in the shredded coconut. Spread the paste over the base of a spring form lined with baking paper and leave to chill.

Cream: Blend cashew nuts, agave syrup, vanilla powder, coconut oil and cocoa butter to a soft cream. Pour the cream into the spring form and leave the cake in the freezer while you prepare the pineapple purée.

Pineapple purée: Blend pineapple, banana, coconut oil and psyllium seed husks and pour over the cake. Place the cake in the freezer for approx. 1 hour until completely set and you can easily remove the sides of the spring form and the baking paper.

Decorate with 'whipped cream' and pineapple/coconut sprinkles.

PINEAPPLE is rich in the anti-inflammatory enzyme bromelain and helps digestion. Pineapple also contains manganese – a mineral which is part of the formation of many enzymes which the body requires for energy production. It is rich in vitamin C, B1 and B2.

Spicy Cake

Do you also dread December's overload of fat and sugar? And are you dreading always having to say no to Christmas temptations? Fear not – here is the recipe which will make you the star of Christmas. Bring this healthy Christmas cake to any party and everyone will think you are the healthiest heroine of Christmas.

Serves approx. 8–10 people

CAKE
125g almonds
125g walnuts
125g hazelnuts
165g dates, stones removed
Juice of ½ orange
Grated zest of 1 orange
2 tsp cinnamon
2 tsp cardamom
3 cloves, finely ground
1 cm piece of ginger, finely grated
1 apple, grated

ORANGE CREAM
60g macadamia nuts, soaked in water
 for 2–3 hours
Juice of 1 orange
Grated zest of ½ orange
1 tbsp agave syrup
1 tbsp lecithin granules

DECORATION
Grated zest of 1 orange

Cake: Grind the almonds finely in a blender or coffee grinder. Chop walnuts and hazelnuts finely. Blend the dates with orange juice to a smooth paste. Add chopped nuts, spices and the grated apple and mix thoroughly. Line a ring form with cling film and spread the paste in the tin. Leave the cake to settle while you prepare the orange cream.

Orange cream: Blend macadamia nuts, orange juice, orange zest, agave syrup and lecithin to a soft cream. Add a little water or more orange juice, if necessary, to blend it well.

Remove the cake from the tin and pour the cream over. Decorate with grated zest of orange.

CINNAMON is used traditionally for the prevention of colds and influenza and to increase appetite and digestion. And it also has antimicrobial and fungicidal properties. Cinnamon also helps to regulate the blood sugar level.

CARDAMOM is an exotic spice which is good for the liver, stomach and digestion. It is used for colds, coughs, bronchitis, as a temperature lowering agent, for gall bladder problems, lack of appetite and strengthens the immune system. In traditional medicine both cardamom and cinnamon are used to improve digestion and to treat bloatedness.

Chocolate Truffle Terrine à la Orange

A festive truffle with orange flavour.

Serves 2

TERRINE
5 medjool dates
1 tablespoon cocoa butter
1 avocado
1 teaspoon psyllium husks
½ teaspoon finely grated zest of an orange
3 tablespoons freshly squeezed orange juice
40g raw cocoa powder
1 tablespoon sunflower lecithin
50 ml almond milk (see page 135)
   (can be substituted with water, if necessary)
3 tablespoons agave syrup, honey or coconut
   syrup

ICING
1 tablespoon coconut butter
1 pinch of turmeric
½ teaspoon agave syrup

Terrine: Remove the stones from the dates and softten them, if necessary, in water. Gently melt the cocoa butter in a bain-marie or place the bowl on a warm radiator. Blend dates, avocado, psyllium husks, zest of orange, raw cocoa powder, melted cocoa butter, sunflower lecithin, almond milk and agave syrup. Pour into a baking tin or similar, lined with cling film, and freeze for 30 minutes. When the terrine has become solid carefully remove from the tin.

Icing: Gently melt the coconut butter in a bowl in a bain-marie. When the coconut butter has completely melted add turmeric and agave syrup. Decorate the terrine with the yellow chocolate icing. Serve with lots of fruit and fresh berries.

AVOCADO is full of the antioxidant vitamin E which among other things strengthens circulation and contributes to keeping your skin beautiful. At the same time avocado is full of carotenoids, for example lutein know for strengthening the eyes. Avocado also has a very high plant sterol content namely beta-sitosterol, campesterol and stigmasterol which are important for the body to keep inflammation under control. These plant sterols have proven to be especially beneficial in the treatment of arthriitis and high cholesterol. Avocado is rich on Omega 9 (oil acid) which lowers cholesterol, keeps skin beautiful and helps to take up the fat soluble vitamins A,D,E and K.

Caramel Cake with Coconut Sprinkles

Sweet caramel is fantastic with coconut. Enjoy it in small delicious morsels which will satisfy all your caramel cravings.

Serves 5

CARAMEL CAKE
120g cashew nuts
30g macadamia nuts
7 medjool dates
1 tablespoon coconut oil
1 tablespoon lucuma powder
1 tablespoon mesquite

SPRINKLES
60g coconut flour (fine)
2 tablespoons coconut sugar
1 teaspoon coconut oil
½ teaspoon vanilla powder

Caramel cake: Grind the cashew nuts finely in a food processor or coffee grinder. Chop the macadamia nuts coarsely. Mash the dates with your hands until you have a soft paste, then add coconut oil, lucuma, mesquite, cashew nut flour and finally the chopped macadamia nuts. Scoop the mixture into a brownie tin and leave it to cool in the fridge, while you prepare the sprinkles.

Sprinkles: Mix coconut flour with coconut sugar, coconut oil and vanilla powder. Sprinkle the coconut mixture over the cake and enjoy it in good company.

MACADAMIA NUTS are also known as 'the queen of nuts' and are the richest source of mono-unsaturated fats, the same kind of fat found in olive oil. They also contain 1.28 mg of different plant sterols per g oil. A diet rich in mono-unsaturated fats and plant sterols has a positive effect on the circulation and the cholesterol composition in the blood.

Chocolate Cake with Strawberries

A small and juicy cake for sharing.

Serves 2

90g Brazil nuts
8 medjool dates
1 teaspoon coconut oil
40g raw cocoa powder
3 strawberries

DECORATION
1 strawberry

Grind the Brazil nuts to a fine flour in a coffee grinder or food processor. Remove the stones from the dates and knead them to a soft paste. Add coconut oil, Brazil nut flour and raw cocoa powder and knead to an even paste. Divide the mixture into two portions and shape into two small round cakes. You could use a mousse ring to keep the shape. Chop the strawberries finely and pile over one chocolate base. Place the other chocolate cake as a lid over the strawberries. Leave the cake in the freezer for approx. 30 minutes until set well enough to stand on its own.

Decorate with strawberries and serve.

Extravagant Chocolate Cake with Butter Cream

A rich treat which will satisfy any craving for chocolate cake – wonderful for festive occasions!

Serves 8–12

SPONGE
5 medjool dates
60g coconut flour (fine)
1 teaspoon coconut oil
1 tablespoon raw cocoa powder
1 tablespoon raw cocoa nibs

BUTTER CREAM
3 tablespoons cocoa butter
5 tablespoons coconut butter
2 tablespoons agave syrup
1 teaspoon sunflower lecithin
1 pinch salt

CHOCOLATE FILLING
7 medjool dates
60g coconut flour (fine)
5 tablespoons raw cocoa powder
4 tablespoons coconut sugar
2 tablespoons coconut oil

CHOCOLATE ICING
3 tablespoons cocoa butter
1 tablespoon sunflower lecithin
1 tablespoon agave syrup or coconut syrup
1 tablespoon raw cocoa powder

Sponge: Remove the stones from the dates and mash them to a soft paste. Add coconut flour, coconut oil, raw cocoa powder and raw cocoa nibs. Knead thoroughly. Line a spring form with baking paper. Spoon the mixture over the base of the spring form.

Butter cream: Gently melt cocoa butter and coconut butter in a bowl in a bain-marie. Add agave syrup, sunflower lecithin and salt. Mix thoroughly. Spread half of the butter cream over the sponge and leave the cake to chill in the fridge.

Chocolate filling: Remove the stones from the dates and mash them to a soft paste. Knead with coconut flour, raw cocoa powder, coconut sugar and coconut oil. The mixture should be crumbly. Spread half of the chocolate over the cake which has been previously chilled. Spread the rest of the butter cream over it, spoon the rest of the chocolate on top of the butter cream. Put the cake in the fridge to chill.

Chocolate icing: Gently melt the cocoa butter in a bain-marie. Add sunflower lecithin, agave syrup and cocoa powder and mix it thoroughly. Carefully remove the cake from the spring form and put it on a plate. Pour the chocolate icing over the cake and serve – preferably with fresh fruit.

Tarts

You little tart, yes you!

Blueberry Tartlets

Small dishes with a taste of marzipan, sweet cream and fresh acidic blueberries.

3 small tartlets or 2 big ones

TART BASE
60g cashew nuts
65g almonds
1 tbsp coconut oil
4 dates, stones removed
A little salt

FILLING
Vanilla cream (see page 139)
200g fresh blueberries

Tart base: Grind cashew nuts and almonds finely in a blender or coffee grinder. Blend the ground nuts with oil, salt and dates and mix to a firm paste. Line an individual tartlet tin with cling film and spread the paste in the tin. When you have shaped a tart from the paste, loosen the cling film and your nut tartlet can now be easily removed. Repeat with the remainder of the paste. Place the tartlets in the freezer for 15 minutes while you prepare the vanilla cream.

Filling: Fold the fresh blueberries into the vanilla cream. The tartlet can now be filled with the blueberry vanilla cream.

BLUEBERRIES contain chrome which helps to regulate the blood sugar. They also contain vitamins B2, C and E, beta-carotene, folate and fibre.

Peach Pie

A fresh peach tart.

Serves approx. 16 people

TART BASE
180g nuts
85g dates, stones removed
A little sea salt
1 tsp vanilla powder
2 tbsp flax seed oil

FILLING
Vanilla cream (see page 139)
3–4 peaches cut into quarters

Tart base: Grind the nuts finely in a blender or coffee grinder. Blend the dates to a uniform paste and mix with the ground nuts, salt, vanilla powder and flax seed oil. Spread the paste into a tart dish. If you don't have a dish with a removable base you can line it with cling film before filling it with the paste. Then it is easier to remove the finished tart. Leave the tart base to chill while you prepare the vanilla cream.

Filling: Spread the vanilla cream over the tart base and top with peaches cut into quarters.

Serve with 'whipped cream' (see page 141) and caramel sauce.

PEACHES contain beta-carotene, folate and vitamin C. Beta-carotene or provitamin A is an efficient antioxidant, important for sight and an important protective agent for the skin while sunbathing. Vitamin C is also an antioxidant which strengthens connective tissue and keeps our skin firm.

Pink Pie

A truly pink lady tart of a sweety pie.

Serves approx. 16 people

TART BASE
300g mixed almonds and cashew nuts
1 tbsp cocoa butter
1 tbsp coconut oil
250g dates, stones removed
2 tbsp raw cocoa powder
1 tbsp agave syrup or raw honey
1 tbsp water
A little shredded coconut

PINK CREAM
2 large bananas
1 tsp vanilla powder
2 tbsp lecithin granules
A little agave syrup or raw honey if you
   have a very sweet tooth
2 tbsp coconut oil
200g frozen strawberries

DECORATION
Fresh strawberries for decoration

Tart base: Grind the almonds in a food processor or blender, and then add cocoa butter and coconut oil. Blend and then add dates, cocoa powder, agave syrup and water. Sprinkle shredded coconut over a tart dish and spread the tart paste over the dish. Leave to rest for approx. 30 minutes in the fridge or freezer while you prepare the filling.

Pink cream: Peel the bananas and blend until creamy with the vanilla powder, lecithin granules, agave syrup or honey and coconut oil. Finally add the frozen strawberries and blend to a thick ice cream. Spread the filling over the tart base and serve immediately, for example with fresh strawberries.

STRAWBERRIES are packed with vitamin C and like other berries contain ellagic acid, a powerful antioxidant. At the same time ellagic acid helps to break down and excrete waste matter. Strawberries have a large content of B3 and B5 which protect the nervous system and are rich in flavonoids.

Papaya Pie

Papaya is super healthy and the tart is so delicious that it will be suitable both for dessert and for breakfast.

Serves approx. 16 people

TART BASE
100g almonds, soaked in water for
  approx. 3 hours
90g walnuts, soaked in water for
  approx. 3 hours
85g dates, stones removed
A little shredded coconut, if necessary

PAPAYA FILLING
2 papayas
2 bananas
2 tsp ground chia seeds
1 ½ tsp lime or lemon juice
1 tsp turmeric

DECORATION
Edible flowers – e.g. cornflowers

Tart base: Blend the almonds and walnuts in a blender or food processor with the dates until they form a firm paste. Spread the paste in a tart dish and leave to chill while you prepare the filling. Sprinkle a little shredded coconut over the base of the tart dish to prevent the tart paste sticking.

Papaya filling: blend papaya, bananas, ground chia seeds, lemon juice and turmeric.

Pour the filling over the tart base. Freeze the tart for 1½ – 2 hours. Cut and serve as dessert or breakfast.

PAPAYA is a good source of vitamin C and beta-carotene. These antioxidants help our immune system and protect against cardiovascular diseases. Papaya contains the enzyme papain which helps digestion of protein and prevents inflammation.

Kïrsch Pie

A crisp base of chocolate filled with soft vanilla cream and juicy cherries.

Serves approx. 16 people

TART BASE
190g almonds
165g dates, stones removed
2 tbsp coconut oil
3 tbsp raw cocoa powder
A little coconut oil for greasing the form

FILLING
200g cherries, stones removed
1 tsp honey, if necessary
Vanilla cream (see page 139)

Tart: Grind the almonds finely in a coffee grinder or a powerful blender. Blend dates and coconut oil to a thick paste and add cocoa powder and ground almonds. Line the tart dish with cling film if you don't have a tart dish with a removable base and fill the chocolate paste into the tart dish. Leave to chill while you prepare the vanilla cream.

Filling: Remove the stones from the cherries and coat them thoroughly with 1 tsp of honey until the cherry juice is released. Pour the vanilla cream over the tart base and top with the cherries.

CHERRIES like many other berries contain ellagic acid, a powerful antioxidant that protects the body cells. They are also packed with anti-inflammatory Vitamin C and strengthen the immune system; they also have a high content of iron of which many women have a deficiency. However the most special characteristic of cherries is their high content of melatonin.

Kiwi Lime Pies

Acidic and green kiwis on a creamy base – fresh and colourful.

Makes approx. 4

TART BASE
85g dates, stones removed
1 tbsp coconut oil
1 tsp hemp seed oil
60g Brazil nuts, finely chopped
100g shredded coconut
1 pinch sea salt

LIME FILLING
2 ripe avocados (or 1 ripe jumbo avocado)
3 tbsp lime juice
50 ml agave syrup
2 tsp finely ground chia seeds (can be replaced by psyllium seed husks)

DECORATION
2 kiwi fruits cut into slices
Lime peel sliced julienne style for decoration

Tart base: Blend dates, coconut oil and hemp seed oil, then add the chopped Brazil nuts, shredded coconut and finally sea salt. Line the tart dishes with cling film and press the tart base into the dish.

Lime filling: Blend the avocados, lime juice, agave syrup and finely ground chia seeds and pour the filling over the tart bases. Leave the tarts to chill while the chia seeds give the filling a blancmange like consistency. Freeze the tarts and remove from the tart dishes before serving.

Decorate the tart with kiwi and peel of lime.

KIWI FRUITS have a high content of vitamin C and have the capacity to retain vitamin C even long after being harvested. **LIME FRUITS** also contain a lot of vitamin C and have a high content of B9, calcium and potassium.

Strawberry Tarts

Tiny delicious strawberry tarts – just like granny used to make them (almost).

Makes approx. 4

TART BASE
190g almonds
10 dates, stones removed, soaked in water
   and mashed
2 tsp coconut oil
1 tsp vanilla powder

FILLING
Vanilla cream (see page 139)

DECORATION
250g fresh strawberries, cut in half and
   stalk removed
Chocolate sauce (see page 136)

Tart base: Grind the almonds finely. Blend dates, coconut oil, vanilla powder and then mix in the ground almonds. Shape the paste in the small tart dishes lined with cling film. The paste should be thick and firm enough to be able to stand up when you remove the finished pastry from the dish. Chill the tart bases in the freezer or fridge.

Filling and decoration: Fill the tart bases with vanilla cream and top with strawberries cut in half. Finally decorate with chocolate sauce.

Apple Tart with Cinnamon

A classic autumn tart. Should be enjoyed wearing a warm pullover and holding a mug of hot tea in the light of candles.

Serves approx. 16 people

TART BASE
125g almonds
60g Brazil nuts
7 dates, stones removed
1 pinch Himalayan salt
1 tbsp flax seed oil
1 tbsp hemp oil

NUT CREAM
120g walnuts, finely ground
6 apricots
1 tsp cinnamon
2 tbsp raw honey
2 tbsp coconut oil
1 pinch Himalayan salt
2 apples cut into thin slices and sprinkled
  with a little lemon juice

CINNAMON OIL
1 tsp cinnamon
1 tbsp raw honey
1 tbsp flax seed oil

Tart base: Grind the almonds and Brazil nuts finely in a coffee grinder. Blend dates with Himalayan salt, flax seed oil and hemp seed oil. Mix in the ground nuts. Line a tart dish with the paste and leave to chill.

Nut cream: Grind the walnuts finely. Blend ground nuts, apricots, cinnamon, honey, coconut oil and Himalayan salt. Fill the tart base and decorate with the apple slices. Mix cinnamon, honey and oil to make cinnamon oil and drizzle over the tart. Leave the tart to chill until serving.

APPLES contain pectin, a food fibre which binds to cholesterol and waste material and excretes it from the body. Pectin also helps to stabilise blood sugar. Apples also contain large quantities of the flavonoid quercetin which is thought to counteract allergies and reduce inflammation. Apple acid improves metabolism and finally apples also contain a lot of vitamin C.

Caramel Tarts

Chocolate and caramel have always been an extremely delicious combination.
Here they are united in a tart which will instantly cure your craving for sweet things.

Makes 3 small tarts

SPONGES
8 medjool dates
3 tablespoons raw cocoa powder
1 tablespoon coconut oil
3 tablespoons coconut flour (fine)

CARAMEL CREAM
10 medjool dates
1 tablespoon mesquite
1 tablespoon lucuma powder
1 teaspoon vanilla powder
1 tablespoon sunflower lecithin
A little water, if needed

Sponges: Remove the stones from the dates
and knead them to a uniform paste with the
raw cocoa powder, coconut oil and coconut
flour. Scoop the paste into three small tart tins
(preferably spring forms with removable bases).
Place the sponges in the fridge while you
prepare the filling.

Caramel cream: Remove the stones from the
dates and blend with mesquite, lucuma powder,
vanilla powder and sunflower lecithin to an even
paste. Add a little water, if necessary, to slacken
it. Spread the caramel cream over the sponges
and place the tarts in the fridge until set.
Carefully remove the tarts from the tins before
serving.

Enjoy with lots of fruit and fresh berries.

Summer Tart

A tart which is incredibly easy to make and which will impress at summer parties.
The tart is an unparalleled spectrum of colours, packed with nutrients, juice and power.

Serves 5

BASE
60g Brazil nuts
60g almonds
7 medjool dates
1 tablespoon coconut oil
1 pinch Himalayan salt
1 teaspoon vanilla powder

CHOCOLATE SAUCE
1 tablespoon cocoa butter
1 tablespoon coconut oil
1 tablespoon agave syrup
2 tablespoons raw cocoa powder

CREAM
2 bananas
1 tablespoon agave syrup
2 tablespoons coconut butter
5 strawberries
2 teaspoons beetroot crystals

FRUIT
3 strawberries
5 green grapes
10 blueberries
1 kiwi
5 cape gooseberries

Base: Grind the Brazil nuts and almonds finely in a coffee grinder or food processor. Knead the nut mixture with the soft dates, coconut oil, salt and vanilla powder. Place the paste in a tart tin.

Chocolate sauce: Gently melt the cocoa butter and coconut oil in a bowl in a bain-marie. When the cocoa butter and coconut oil have completely melted, remove the bowl from the bain-marie. Mix the agave syrup and raw cocoa powder with the chocolate and stir it well. Spoon the chocolate sauce over the base and place in the fridge for 3 minutes while you make the cream.

Cream: Blend bananas, agave syrup, coconut butter, strawberries and beetroot crystals to a soft paste. Pour the cream into the base of the tart tin. Pour lots of colourful fruits and berries over the cream and enjoy the tart in sunshine with good friends.

Brownies

And a whitey!

Brownie Babe

A dark chocolate brownie with sprinkles of orange goji berries. This brownie I invented for Denmark's first raw food cafe 42° RAW.

Makes approx. 16

CAKE PASTRY
10 dates, stones removed
200 ml coconut oil
80g raw cocoa powder
1 pinch Himalayan salt
120g Brazil nuts, coarsely chopped

SPRINKLES
50g goji berries
50g shredded coconut

Cake pastry: Blend dates, coconut oil, cocoa powder and Himalayan salt to a date paste. Add a little water, if necessary. Mix in the chopped Brazil nuts. Shape the pastry to a 3 cm (approx.) thick base in a brownie form (or other similar square baking tray) and leave to chill while you prepare the goji berry sprinkles.

Sprinkles: Blend goji berries and shredded coconut in a blender or coffee grinder and sprinkle over the cake. Cut the cake into squares before serving.

Tip: You can increase the nutritional value of chocolate brownies by adding a couple of tablespoons of maca powder or hemp seeds to the pastry.

BRAZIL NUTS are among the most nutritious nuts available. They contain much of the immune stimulating antioxidant selenium which helps prevent cardiovascular diseases and premature ageing. Selenium is also important for sight and for healthy hair and skin. Brazil nuts contain zinc, magnesium, calcium, glutathione and iron, Omega 6, B1 and biotin and are rich in protein.

Choconutz Brownie with Caramel Topping

A crunchy brownie with a delicious toffee on top.

Makes approx. 16

CAKE PASTRY
85g dates, stones removed
100 ml coconut oil
1 pinch Himalayan salt
80g raw cocoa powder
120g Brazil nuts, coarsely chopped

CARAMEL TOPPING
120g cashew nuts, soaked in water for 2 hours
100 ml water
1 pinch Himalayan salt
2 tbsp lecithin granules
165g dates
1 tbsp lucuma powder
½ tsp vanilla powder

Cake pastry: Blend all the ingredients – except for the Brazil nuts. When the brownie pastry is sufficiently smooth, mix in the Brazil nuts and press the chocolate paste into a square tin or small baking tray lined with cling film or baking paper and leave to chill in freezer or fridge.

Caramel topping: Blend cashew nuts with water, Himalayan salt, lecithin granules, dates, lucuma and vanilla powder using a powerful blender.

When the brownie pastry is set, remove from the tray and top with caramel. You can now cut the brownie into just the right mouth-size bites you want.

Superfood Brownie

A veritable protein bomb which in total contains 66.1g of protein from the hemp seeds, Brazil nuts, raw cocoa powder, bee pollen and goji berries. In comparison 100g beef contains approx. 21g protein.

Serves 4

BROWNIE
12 medjool dates
2 tablespoons coconut oil
40g raw cocoa powder
1 pinch Himalayan salt
60g Brazil nuts
2 tablespoons hemp seeds
2 tablespoons bee pollen
2 tablespoons goji berries

SPRINKLES
50g goji berries
60g coconut flour (fine)

Brownie: Remove the stones from the dates and knead them to a soft, uniform paste. Add coconut oil, raw cocoa powder and salt, and knead thoroughly. Chop the Brazil nuts coarsely and mix with the paste together with the hemp seeds, bee pollen and goji berries. Knead again. Place the mixture in a brownie tin (or other square tin) in a layer, approx. 3 cm thick and leave to cool in the fridge, while you prepare the sprinkles. Serve with fresh raspberries and raspberry coulis (see page 136).

Sprinkles: Blend goji berries and coconut flour in a blender or coffee grinder and sprinkle over the cake. Cut the cake into squares and serve.

BEE POLLEN contains 25% protein and all 22 amino acids which makes it a complete protein. At the same time it contains 18 different vitamins and more than 30 minerals, in particular manganese, lots of enzymes and essential fatty acids.

Whitey

A white chocolate brownie.

Makes approx. 16

CAKE PASTRY
50 ml coconut oil
3 tbsp cocoa butter
60g macadamia nuts, soaked in water
  for 2–3 hours
85g dates, stones removed
1 pinch Himalayan salt
4 tbsp lucuma powder
2 tbsp vanilla powder
120g coarsely chopped Brazil nuts

Cake pastry: Blend coconut oil, cocoa butter and macadamia nuts. Then add dates and mix the date paste with salt, lucuma powder, vanilla powder and the chopped Brazil nuts. Shape the pastry to a 3 cm thick layer in a brownie tin (or other square dish) and leave to chill.

Serve with fresh raspberries and raspberry coulis (see page 136).

Cupcakes

For you, my little cupcake

Cupcakes

Cupcakes can be made in numerous combinations – therefore I will let you compose your own personal raw cupcake. Here you can choose between four different types of cake bases and 12 different types of frosting. Enjoy!

You will get the best bases for cupcakes by shaping them in a muffin baking tray. These are available from many supermarkets and kitchen equipment stockists. Place a colourful paper case in each muffin hollow in the muffin tray and shape the cake pastry in this. This way they will keep their shape.

Chocolate Cupcake

Makes approx. 6 large cupcakes

450g nuts, e.g. almonds
60g raw cocoa powder
125g date paste (see below)

3 tbsp agave syrup
1 tsp vanilla powder

Grind the nuts finely in a blender or coffee grinder. Mix the ingredients thoroughly and fill the muffin tray. Top the cupcakes with differenct icings in beautiful colours, such as the orange icing (see page 104).

DATE PASTE
Date paste for cupcakes is made by blending approx. 200 ml dates with 2–4 tbsp almond milk or coconut milk (see page 135). The coconut milk can be replaced with water and 1 tsp lecithin granules.

Mini Cupcakes
Chocolate with Strawberry Cream

The mixture of the intense and sweet chocolate with the fresh and acidic strawberries is delicious.

Makes approx. 8

CUPCAKES
8 medjool dates
90g Brazil nuts
1 teaspoon coconut oil
60g coconut flour (fine)
40g raw cocoa powder

STRAWBERRY CREAM
2 tablespoons coconut butter
1 banana
60g strawberries, fresh or frozen
1 teaspoon beetroot crystals
1 teaspoon psyllium husks
1 tbsp agave syrup or raw honey, if you
  have a very sweet tooth

Cupcakes: Remove the stones from the dates and mash them to a soft paste. Grind the Brazil nuts in a coffee grinder or food processor. Mix the Brazil nut flour, coconut oil, coconut flour and raw cocoa powder with the date paste. Spoon the chocolate paste into mini-muffin moulds.

Strawberry cream: Blend coconut butter, banana, strawberries, beetroot crystals and psyllium husks. Leave the cream to rest a little while. Spoon it into an icing bag and decorate your chocolate cupcakes with the strawberry cream.

Please note: Frozen strawberries should be defrosted and drained before use.

Mini Cupcakes
Vanilla with Banana Cream

Sweet and delicious cupcakes with the perfect mixture of vanilla and banana.

Makes approx. 8

CUPCAKES
7 medjool dates
100g almonds
1 tablespoon coconut oil
60g coconut flour (fine)
1 teaspoon vanilla powder

BANANA CREAM
2 tablespoons coconut butter
2 bananas
1 teaspoon turmeric
1 teaspoon psyllium husks
2 tablespoons agave syrup

Cupcakes: Remove the stones from the dates and mash them to a soft paste. Grind the almonds to a fine flour in a coffee grinder or food processor. Mix the almond flour, coconut oil, coconut flour and vanilla powder. Spoon the paste into the mini muffin moulds.

Banana cream: Blend coconut butter, bananas turmeric, psyllium husks and agave syrup. Spoon the banana cream into an icing bag to decorate your vanilla cupcakes.

Vanilla Cupcake

Makes approx. 6 large cupcakes

500g nuts, e.g. almonds
6 tsp vanilla powder
125g date paste (see page 96)
2 tbsp agave syrup

Grind the nuts finely in a blender or coffee grinder. Mix the ingredients thoroughly and fill the muffin tray in beautiful colours.

Caramel Cupcake

Makes approx. 6 large cupcakes

500g nuts, e.g. almonds
3 tsp vanilla powder
4 tsp lucuma powder
165g date paste (see page 96)
2 tbsp agave syrup

Grind the nuts finely in a blender or coffee grinder. Mix the ingredients thoroughly and fill the muffin tray in beautiful colours.

Basic Icing for Cupcakes

Makes approx. 6 large cupcakes

175g cashew or macadamia nuts, soaked in
   water for approx. 2–4 hours
4 tbsp agave syrup or raw honey
3 tbsp coconut oil
1 tbsp cocoa butter
2 tbsp lecithin granules
A little water to mix it all more easily

Blend all the ingredients to a soft and
creamy consistency.

Icing-Flavour Variations

ORANGE
Blend 2 tbsp orange juice and 1 tsp grated
zest of orange with basic icing. Add 1½ tsp
dried turmeric to make the cream yellow.

BANANA
Blend a very ripe banana with basic icing.

BLUE MANNA
Blend 3 tsp blue manna and 1 tbsp agave
syrup with basic icing.

CHLORELLA
Blend 2 tsp chlorella and 1 tbsp agave syrup
with basic icing. Add 1 tsp turmeric to turn the
colour vivid green (see photo on page 103)

CHOCOLATE
Blend 2 tbsp raw cocoa powder and 1 tbsp
agave syrup with basic icing.

CREAM CHEESE
Blend 2 tbsp lemon juice and 1 pinch salt with
basic icing.

GOJI BERRIES
Blend 100 ml goji berries previously soaked in
water with basic icing.

STRAWBERRIES
Blend 100 ml fresh or frozen (defrosted)
strawberries with basic icing.

CORNFLOWER
Place 4 tsp dried cornflowers to soak in 4 tsp
water for 10 minutes. Blend with basic icing
and 1 extra tbsp agave syrup.

LUCUMA CARAMEL
Blend 4 soft dates with 2 tsp lucuma powder
with basic icing.

MINT
Blend 100 ml fresh mint leaves, 2 drops of
peppermint oil and 1 tbsp agave syrup with
basic icing. Works particularly well with
chocolate cupcakes.

PEANUT BUTTER
Blend 100 ml Jungle Peanuts previously
soaked in water for approx. 3 hours with 100
ml agave syrup and basic icing.

VANILLA
Blend 3 tsp vanilla powder with basic icing.

Cookies

You think you are a
tough cookie?

Ginger Cookie

To make completely crisp cookies you must have a dehydrator which dries the cookies.
If you are not the lucky owner of such a dehydrator you can roll the cookies to juicy balls
instead – they are not crisp, but definitely just as delicious in this way.

Makes approx. 20

400g dates, stones removed
3 cm piece ginger, finely grated
1 pinch Himalayan salt
2 tbsp agave syrup
400g shredded coconut

Blend dates, ginger, salt and agave syrup to a smooth paste. Add a little water to make it easier to mix. Thoroughly mix the date paste with shredded coconut and roll out the pastry to approx. $\frac{1}{2}$ cm thick. Cut out the cookies with a biscuit cutter or use a glass with a very thin rim, e.g. a champagne glass. Place the cookies on the dehydrator trays and dry for approx. 8–10 hours. The cakes will keep in an airtight container for up to 4–6 weeks (if you can keep your fingers away from them for that long.)

Tip: Before you roll out the sticky pastry it is a good idea to place a piece of baking paper underneath and on top of the pastry. This way it will not stick to the table top or the rolling pin.

GINGER is used both to treat colds and influenza, digestive problems and to relieve nausea in motion sickness or pregnancy. Ginger strengthens circulation and relieves pain and inflammation.

Sheriff Stars

Funny, small cookies and a fantastic idea for festive occasions.

Serves 7

SHERIFF STARS
100g almonds
90g Brazil nuts
60g coconut flour (fine)
3 tablespoons coconut sugar
9 medjool dates
3 tablespoons coconut oil
1 teaspoon vanilla powder

STAR DUST CREAM
40g cocoa butter
2 tablespoons coconut butter
1 teaspoon sunflower lecithin
$\frac{1}{2}$ tsp turmeric
1 teaspoon agave syrup

Sheriff stars: Grind almonds and Brazil nuts finely in a coffee grinder or food processor. Pour into a bowl and mix with coconut flour and coconut sugar. Remove the stones from the dates and knead them to a soft paste. Mix the nut flour with the date paste. Add coconut oil and vanilla powder and knead thoroughly. Roll out the paste on a piece of baking paper to a thickness of approx. $\frac{1}{2}$ cm. Cut out stars with a biscuit cutter. Leave the stars to firm up while you prepare the cream.

Star dust cream: Gently melt the cocoa butter and coconut butter in a bowl in a bain-marie, until completely melted. Add sunflower lecithin, turmeric and agave syrup. Stir the cream well until it is a uniform colour. Coat the stars with the cream and keep cool until serving.

Lemon-Coco Cookie

Makes approx. 20

400g dates, stones removed
Grated peel of an organic lemon
Juice of ½ lemon
1 pinch Himalayan salt
2 tbsp agave syrup
400g shredded coconut

Blend dates, lemon, salt and agave syrup to a smooth paste. Add a little water, if necessary, to make it easier to mix. Thoroughly mix the paste with shredded coconut and roll the pastry out to approx. ½ cm thick. Cut out the biscuits with either a biscuit cutter or use a glass with a very thin rim, e.g. a champagne glass. Place the biscuits on the dehydrator trays and dry for approx. 8–10 hours. Will keep in an airtight container for up to approx. 4–6 weeks.

LEMON In the peel of the lemon there is a substance called limonene which has anti-septic and antibacterial properties. Limonene is therefore also often used in cleaning products.

Choco-Crunch Cookie

Makes approx. 20

350g Brazil nuts
250g almonds
500g dates, stones removed
50 ml almond milk (see page 135)
1 pinch Himalayan salt
5 tbsp agave syrup
40g raw cocoa powder
30g raw cocoa nibs

Grind Brazil nuts and almonds finely in a blender or coffee grinder. Blend dates, almond milk, salt and agave syrup to a smooth paste. Thoroughly mix the date paste with the ground nuts, cocoa powder, cocoa nibs and roll out the pastry to a thickness of approx. $\frac{1}{2}$ cm. Cut the cookies either with a biscuit cutter or use a glass with a very thin rim such as a champagne glass. Place the cookies on ParaFlexx sheets or baking paper and dry them in the dehydrator for approx. 8–10 hours. Can be kept in an airtight container for up to 4–6 weeks.

Caramel Cookie

Makes approx. 20

350g Brazil nuts
375g almonds
500g dates, stones removed
100 ml almond milk (see page 135)
1 pinch Himalayan salt
3 tbsp agave syrup
4 tbsp lucuma powder
3 tbsp vanilla powder

Grind the Brazil nuts and almonds finely in a blender or coffee grinder. Blend dates, almond milk, salt and agave syrup to a smooth paste. Thoroughly mix the date paste with the ground nuts, lucuma and vanilla powder and roll it out to a thickness of approx. $\frac{1}{2}$ cm. Cut the cookies either with a biscuit cutter or use a glass with a very thin rim, e.g. a champagne glass. Place the cookies on ParaFlexx sheets or baking paper and dry them in the dehydrator for approx. 8–10 hours. Can be kept in an airtight container for up to approx. 4–6 weeks.

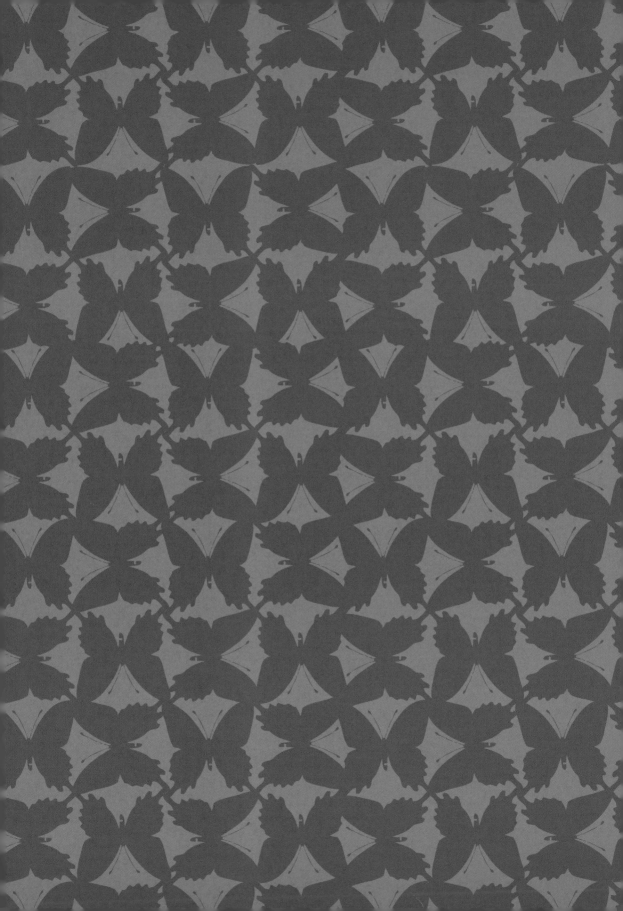

Ice cream

I scream, you scream,
we all scream for
RAW ice cream!

Mango Sorbet

A fresh sorbet which can be made in two minutes.

YOU WILL NEED PER PERSON
80g frozen mango cut into pieces
A little agave syrup or honey, if you have a very
  sweet tooth

Blend the frozen mango – with a little agave syrup, if needed, – until it becomes completely creamy and sorbet like.

Enjoy the sorbet in beautiful glasses. Decorate with super foods e.g. raw cocoa nibs, inca- and goji berries.

Goji Strawberry Granita

A super simple ice cream with an extra health kick and crunch from the goji berries.

YOU WILL NEED PER PERSON
80g frozen strawberries
½ handful goji berries
**A little agave syrup or honey, if you have a very
  sweet tooth**

TOPPING
Goji berries
Raw cocoa nibs

Blend all ingredients to make a cracking ice cream. Serve the sorbet in beautiful glasses. Sprinkle with your favourite super food, e.g. raw cocoa nibs, goji berries and mulberries.

N'ice Cream

One more super easy ice cream dish using banana – but with an extravagant topping.
A real Sundae ice cream.

YOU WILL NEED PER PERSON
2 frozen bananas
1 tsp agave syrup
1 tsp coconut oil

TOPPING
Chocolate sauce (see page 136),
  super foods and fresh berries

Blend bananas, agave syrup and coconut oil to a creamy texture. Arrange in individual glasses, and pour over the chocolate sauce in generous quantity. Sprinkle with your favourite super food, for example goji berries, and raw cocoa nibs and fresh fruit.

Matcha Ice Cream

An ice-cold energy bomb filled with green tea.

YOU WILL NEED PER PERSON
80g frozen pineapple
1 tsp matcha powder
2 tsp agave syrup

TOPPING
Goji berries

Blend frozen pineapple with matcha powder and agave syrup until the mixture is creamy. Serve in glasses and sprinkle with goji berries.

MATCHA TEA is the tea used in the traditional Japanese tea ceremony. The ritual builds on four basic principles, harmony, respect, purity and inner peace. Matcha is one of the finest leaves from the first harvest of the year. A special cultivation process means that the leaves will have a more concentrated chlorophyll content, giving the tea the vivid green colour and a finer aroma compared to regular green tea. The dry leaves are ground in a stone mill to a fine powder. Matcha has a stimulating effect and is thicker than regular green tea. Since you drink the leaves they provide the body with a very high dose of vitamins A, C and E and minerals and antioxidants, including catechins.

Vanilla Ice Cream

'Ice cream' made on the basis of nuts has a much lighter texture than ordinary ice cream, it is rounder and milder.

Serves approx. 4 people

120g cashew or macadamia nuts
150 ml water
3 tbsp agave syrup
2 tsp vanilla powder
2 tbsp lecithin granules

Blend all ingredients and chill the cream in the fridge. Pour the chilled cream into your ice-cream maker and follow the instructions. If you are not the lucky owner of an ice-cream machine you can just freeze the cream for approx. 4 hours – but stir it regularly every 20 minutes or so, until it is frozen. If it is still too hard you can make it creamy again by putting it through a food processor.

Chocolate Ice Cream

Serves approx. 4 people

120g cashew or macadamia nuts
150 ml water
3 tbsp agave syrup
2 tsp vanilla powder
2 tbsp lecithin granules
4 tbsp raw cocoa powder
3 tbsp agave syrup

Use the same method as for making vanilla ice cream in the previous recipe. Add raw cocoa powder and agave syrup before freezing it.

Ice Cream Burger

This is a self assembly recipe.

1. Choose your favourite cookie
(For this recipe it is not a problem if you do not have a dehydrator. Just shape it as a cookie – it will set in the freezer anyway.)

2. Choose your favourite ice cream
(However, please note that matcha ice cream is not suitable for this recipe.)

3. Place a good helping of ice cream between the two cookies

4. Freeze

5. Enjoy

Ice Boats

Like the ice cream burgers, the ice boats make a self assembly set of recipes.

1. Choose your favourite tart, pie or tartlet base.

2. Shape it in your chosen tin – first line the tin with cling film , since this will make it easier to remove the pastry when ready.

3. Choose your favourite ice cream.

4. Fill the base of the boat with as much ice cream as possible.

5. Pour over an extravagant layer of chocolate sauce (see page 136).

6. Enjoy immediately – or freeze for later enjoyment.

Extras

Extra! Extra! Read all about it!

Almond Milk

20 almonds
10 cashew nuts
1 litre water
3 tsp lecithin granules
1 tsp agave syrup
1 pinch Himalayan salt

Blend all ingredients. Pass the almond pulp through a sieve and set aside, serve the milk ice cold and enjoy.

Coconut Milk

Coconut milk
150g shredded coconut
300 ml water

Blend in a powerful blender – pass through a sieve, if necessary. .

Caramel Sauce

165g dates, stones removed
150 ml water
2 tsp agave syrup
1 tbsp lecithin granules
2 tsp vanilla powder

Blend all ingredients – add a little more water, if you want a slightly thinner consistency.

Raspberry Coulis

120g raspberries
2 tbsp agave syrup

Blend all ingredients.

Chocolate Sauce

85g dates, stones removed
150 ml water
3 tbsp raw cocoa powder
1 tbsp coconut oil

Blend ingredients – add a little more water if you want a slightly thinner consistency.

Vanilla Cream

100 ml water
3 tbsp agave syrup
2 tsp vanilla powder
2 tbsp lecithin granules

Blend all ingredients.

Vanilla Cream Light

3 ripe bananas
2 tsp vanilla powder
2 tbsp lecithin granules
A little more water, if necessary

Blend all ingredients.

'Whipped Cream'

120g cashew or macadamia nuts, soaked in
  water for at least 2 hours
100 ml water
2 tbsp coconut oil or cocoa butter
2 tbsp agave syrup
1 tsp vanilla powder
2 tbsp lecithin granules
2 tsp psyllium seed husks

Blend all ingredients. Pour the cream into a
container and chill in the fridge or freezer. When
the cream is thoroughly chilled, blend for 30
seconds to make it lighter.

Stockists and Links

Luckily the supply of super foods and raw goods gets better all the time – especially if you are able to shop online – and almost any self-respecting health food shop will also stock a decent range of raw food goods. Here are some of my favourite suppliers:

AUSTRALIA
https://raw-pleasure.com.au/
The Raw Food Store is Australia's newest online raw food store.

CANADA
https://realrawfood.com
Distributor of organically grown raw foods.

www.rawnutrition.ca
Raw foods, supplements and equipment.

SOUTH AFRICA
http://www.superfoods.co.za/
Raw foods, equipment and supplements.

UK
www.rawliving.eu
This is the online shop run by Kate Magic, whose two books *Eat Smart Eat Raw* and *Raw Living* are also published by Grub Street.

www.aardvark-wholefoods.com
A bricks and mortar shop in Carmarthen, South Wales with online shop.

www.earthfare.co.uk
A bricks and mortar shop in Glastonbury, Somerset, England with extensive raw food products online.

www.funkyraw.com
Online shop is a supplier of raw foods and super foods in the UK and Europe.

www.planetorganic.com
The UK's largest organic supermarket. They ship all the products on their website worldwide.

www.rawhealth.uk.com
Offering range of raw chocolate and raw snacks. Useful directory of shops and online stockists of raw and vegan foods.

www.realfoods.co.uk
Two bricks and mortar shops in Edinburgh with extensive range of super foods online.

www.wholefoodsmarkets.com
The supermarket chain with branches in the US, Canada and the UK. An enormous range of raw food products.

USA
www.rawguru.com
Store, blog and newsletter.

www.allrawdirectory.com
One stop shop directory for everything relating to raw lifestyle.

READ MORE ABOUT RAW FOOD:

www.carolinefibaek.eu
My own website, where you can keep up to date with lectures, courses and workshops and read more about my consultations. On the blog you will find lots of inspiration and recipes.

www.hippocratesinst.com
The oldest centre for the treatment with raw food and complementary medicine managed by doctors. Brian and Anna Maria Clement.

www.anoasisofhealing.com
Dr. Thomas Lodi is a specialist in complementary medicine and treatments and raw food lecturer.

Index

Thanks

A PERSONAL THANK YOU TO

MR.MAN AKA COOKIEMONSTER – thank you for sparring, patience and evaluation of all the recipes, you are a true connoisseur! You are my own personal guru – thank you for your magic. Together we throw dreams towards the sky and fall towards the stars.

MR. T MY OWN LITTLE CUPCAKE
Thank you for showing me the way.

SØREN FLAMMEN WOLF from rawfood.dk – for introducing me to raw food!

I am grateful for being allowed to join in the creation of Denmark's first raw food restaurant **42° RAW**. Thank you **Jesper**, for making raw food easily available for everyone.

THE LOVELY LADIES ANNE AND TINE from Raw and More for sponsoring exotic ingredients and ecstatic super foods for the cake photos.

THE GIRLS IN UKRUDT Anne Line and Sofie – because you so willingly turn up with deliveries, and for your deep and genuine engagement in making the world more sustainable and organic. If only all grocers were like you!

SOFIE – my fantastic graphic designer and cake stylist – thank you for the lovely though hectic times over maca and raw cocoa. We should have a lot more of those!

TURE – the world's coolest photographer. Thank you for putting up with our girly universe!

Visit Sofie and Ture's flowing, creative and sustainable studio on www.ouro.dk

PROPS – thank you for generously lending dishes and plates from Fil de Fer, Susanne Dyhre Poulsen and Royal Copenhagen.

And thank you to my entire self-chosen family, because you are here – you know yourselves who you are, for you are holding a signed copy of this book.

NAMASTE